Mexico
or Bust!

Deborah Underwood

Chicago, Illinois

© 2008 Raintree
Published by Raintree,
A division of Reed Elsevier Inc.
Chicago, Illinois

Customer Service 888-454-2279

Visit our website at www.heinemannraintree.com

Designed by Philippa Jenkins and Q2A Creative

Printed by Leo Paper Group

12 11 10 09 08
10 9 8 7 6 5 4 3 2 1

Library of Congress Cataloging-in-Publication Data
Underwood, Deborah.
  Mexico or bust / Deborah Underwood.
    p. cm.
  Includes bibliographical references.
  ISBN-13: 978-1-4109-2842-9 (library binding)
  ISBN-10: 1-4109-2842-X (library binding)
  ISBN-13: 978-1-4109-2859-7 (pbk.)
  ISBN-10: 1-4109-2859-4 (pbk.)
1. Monarch butterfly--Migration--Juvenile literature.
I. Title.
  QL561.D3U53 2007
  595.78'9--dc22
                                        2006102042

Acknowledgments
The author and publisher are grateful to the following for permission to reproduce copyright material: Ardea pp. **7** (Chris Harvey), **10** (B. Moose Peterson), **13** (Francois Gohier); Corbis pp. **16** (Danny Lehman), **21** (W. Perry Conway), **23** (Dan Guravich), **27** (Darrell Gulin); FLPA p. **14** (Fritz Polking); FLPA/Minden Pictures pp. **4** (Frans Lanting), **8–9** (Suzi Eszterhas), **12–13** (Larry Minden); Getty Images/Aurora p. **18–19** (Peter Essick); Oxford Scientific p. **6**; Oxford Scientific Films p. **24** (Brian Kenney); Oxford Scientific/Animals Animals/Earth Scenes p. **15** (Shane Moore), **25** (Willard Luce); Photolibrary.com/Photographer's Choice p. **5** (Connie Coleman).

Cover photograph of monarch butterflies in Mexico reproduced with permission of Corbis/Danny Lehman.

Illustrations by Jeff Edwards.

The publishers would like to thank Nancy Harris and Harold Pratt for their assistance in the preparation of this book.

Every effort has been made to contact copyright holders of any material reproduced in this book. Any omissions will be rectified in subsequent printings if notice is given to the publishers.

Disclaimer
All the Internet addresses (URLs) given in this book were valid at the time of going to press. However, due to the dynamic nature of the Internet, some addresses may have changed, or sites may have changed or ceased to exist since publication. While the author and publishers regret any inconvenience this may cause readers, no responsibility for any such changes can be accepted by either the author or the publishers.

It is recommended that adults supervise children on the Internet.

Contents

Some words are printed in bold, **like this**. You can find out what they mean on page 30. You can also look in the box at the bottom of the page where they first appear.

Special Butterflies

Late summer sun streams into a garden. The garden is in Canada (see map on page 11). A small green shape hangs from a plant. The shape is called a **chrysalis**. A chrysalis is what a caterpillar becomes. The chrysalis will turn into a butterfly.

The chrysalis turns dark. The next day it splits open. The butterfly **emerges** (comes out). Soon it can fly through the garden.

A monarch chrysalis is green and gold.

chrysalis   stage of life between caterpillar and butterfly
emerge   come out
monarch   type of orange-and-black butterfly

Monarch wings look like stained glass.

This butterfly is a **monarch**. A monarch's wings are orange and black.

Most monarchs live for only a month or so. But monarchs that come out in late summer are special. They can live as long as nine months. Their long lives let them make a long journey.

Each fall these monarchs leave their homes. Some travel to California's coasts. Most fly to forests in Mexico (see map on page 11).

5

Animal Trips

Some animals **migrate**. That means they travel away from their homes and back again. Not all animals migrate. But many do. They travel by land, sea, and sky. Some small insects migrate. So do huge whales.

An animal may make just one trip in its life. Other animals make trips every year. Many birds fly south for the winter. In the spring, they fly north again.

Pacific salmon may swim 2,500 miles (4,023 kilometers) to get home.

migrate   travel away from home and back again

Watching birds migrate is a treat for bird lovers.

Some tiny sea animals migrate each day. They stay deep in the ocean while the Sun shines. At night they swim up near the water's surface. They keep out of the light. This makes it hard for other animals to hunt them.

Migrating salmon

Pacific salmon eggs hatch in streams. The newly hatched fish swim to the ocean. They may live there for years. Then, they swim back to where they were born. They lay eggs there before they die.

Why Migrate?

Animals that **migrate** travel from their homes and back again. They may go thousands of miles. Traveling can be hard work. But animals have good reasons to migrate.

Some animals migrate to find food. Each year animals called wildebeest migrate. They live in Africa. They travel to find fresh grasses. When food runs out, they move to another spot.

↓ *Each year more than one million wildebeest migrate.*

breed have offspring

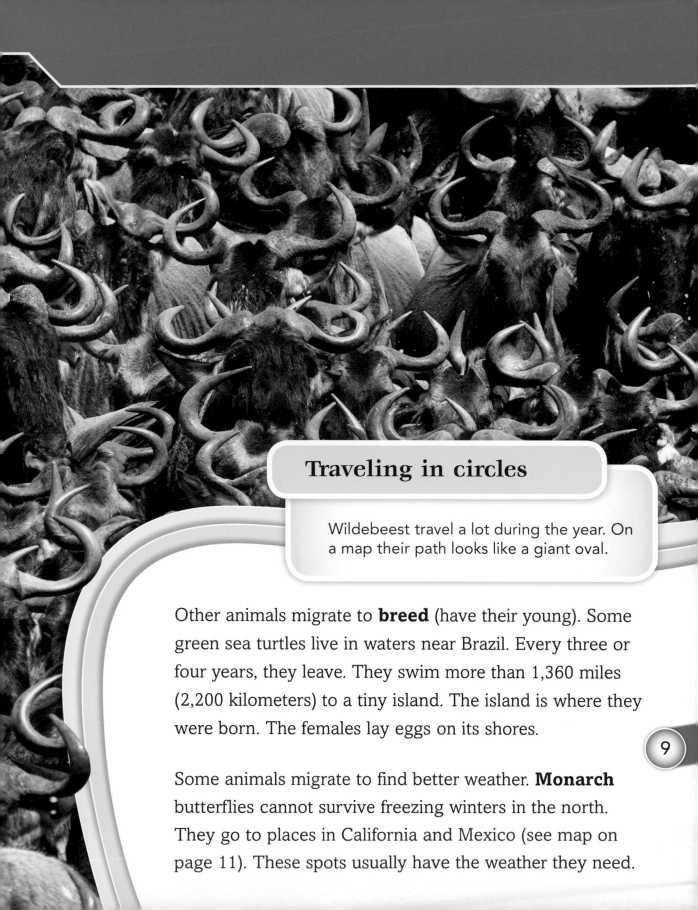

Traveling in circles

Wildebeest travel a lot during the year. On a map their path looks like a giant oval.

Other animals migrate to **breed** (have their young). Some green sea turtles live in waters near Brazil. Every three or four years, they leave. They swim more than 1,360 miles (2,200 kilometers) to a tiny island. The island is where they were born. The females lay eggs on its shores.

Some animals migrate to find better weather. **Monarch** butterflies cannot survive freezing winters in the north. They go to places in California and Mexico (see map on page 11). These spots usually have the weather they need.

Time to fly

As summer ends, days get shorter. The air grows colder. These things bring about changes in the **monarchs**.

Monarch butterflies usually **mate** soon after they **emerge** (come out). Males and females join together. Then, females lay eggs. But late-summer monarchs are different. They do not mate right away. They prepare for a long trip.

Monarchs make long journeys. But birds called arctic terns fly even farther.

Long journey

Arctic terns travel from the Arctic to Antarctica and back. They may travel 22,000 miles (35,405 kilometers) in a year!

Arctic tern

mate   join together to have offspring

Most North American monarchs live east of the Rocky Mountains (see map). They travel to Mexico for the winter.

Some monarchs live west of the Rocky Mountains. Most of them **migrate** to California. They spend the winter in trees by the ocean.

The monarch drinks from flowers. She grows strong. One day her body tells her it is time to leave. She flies south from Canada (see map). She will never return north. But with luck, her children will.

Follow these maps throughout the book to see one monarch's journey from Canada to Mexico.

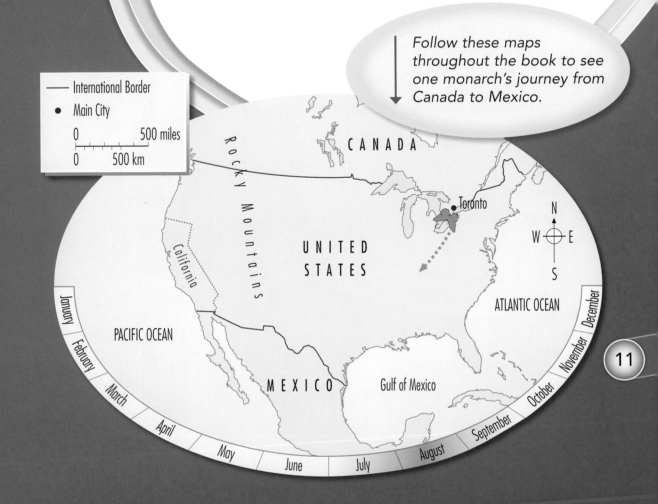

International Border

Main City

0   500 miles
0   500 km

CANADA

Rocky Mountains

Toronto

California

UNITED STATES

N
W   E
S

ATLANTIC OCEAN

PACIFIC OCEAN

MEXICO   Gulf of Mexico

January
February
March
April
May
June
July
August
September
October
November
December

Monarch Mystery

For many years, scientists did not know that **monarchs** fly to Mexico. Each fall people saw the monarchs flying away. Where did they go? Solving this puzzle took 40 years.

It is easy to chase a butterfly for a moment. But chasing it for three months is another matter! Monarchs can travel thousands of feet above the ground. People needed a way to track them.

Tags like this one help scientists learn where monarchs go.

In the 1930s two people found a way to track monarchs. Dr. Fred Urquhart and his wife, Nora, began to **tag** monarchs. They put small labels on the monarchs' wings. Each label had a number on it. Then, they freed the monarchs.

tag put a marker on an animal or insect to find out where it travels

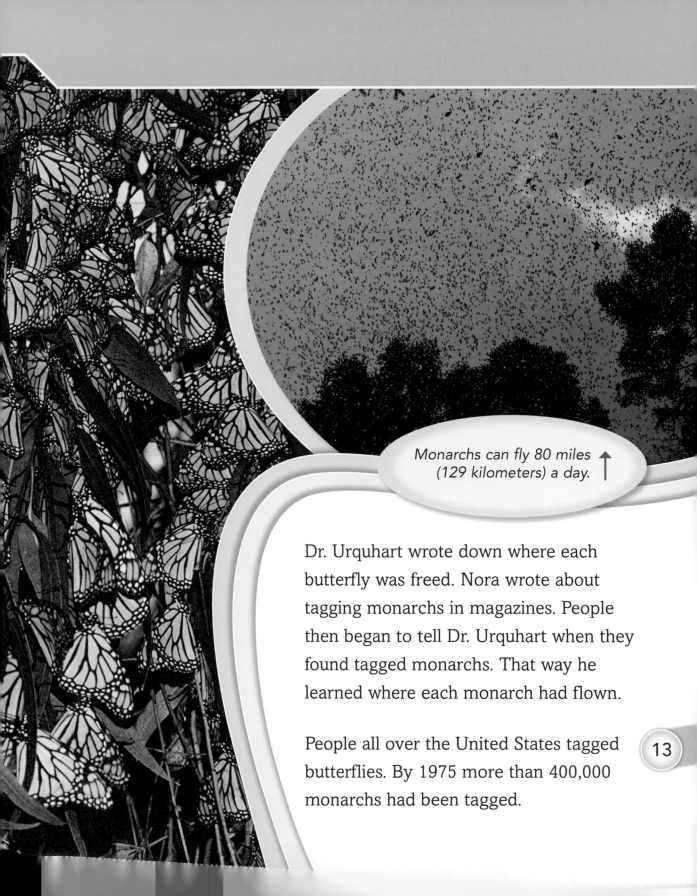

Monarchs can fly 80 miles (129 kilometers) a day. ↑

Dr. Urquhart wrote down where each butterfly was freed. Nora wrote about tagging monarchs in magazines. People then began to tell Dr. Urquhart when they found tagged monarchs. That way he learned where each monarch had flown.

People all over the United States tagged butterflies. By 1975 more than 400,000 monarchs had been tagged.

Tracking Monarchs

Dr. Urquhart collected a lot of information. He charted **monarch** trips on a map. Their paths pointed to Mexico. But where in Mexico did they go?

Ken Brugger and Catalina Aguado helped Dr. Urquhart. They searched for the monarchs in Mexico. Other people who lived there helped. They told the pair where monarchs had been seen.

Most monarchs spend the winter in Mexican forests.

Sometimes scientists use high-tech tools to track animals. This elk wears a special collar. The collar sends a signal back to scientists. They use the signal to find the elk.

In 1975 Brugger and Aguado were climbing a mountain peak. They saw a monarch in the air. They followed it to a spot in the forest. Millions of monarchs covered the trees. The mystery was solved! Other butterfly areas were found nearby.

The next year Urquhart found a **tagged** monarch in Mexico. The monarch had been tagged in Minnesota. This proved that monarchs could make this long trip.

Finding the way

The **monarchs** fly to a small part of Mexico (see map). They start to arrive in October. They clump together in about a dozen places. Monarchs can be found in the same spots each year. They often fly to the same trees monarchs used in past years.

Each monarch travels to Mexico just once. There are no other monarchs alive who can teach them the way. Why do they not get lost?

Monarchs do not need to be shown the way. The tools they need are in their bodies. Monarchs use the Sun to help guide them. They also have a kind of clock in their brains. It helps keep them on track.

These monarchs are covering the branches of a tree.

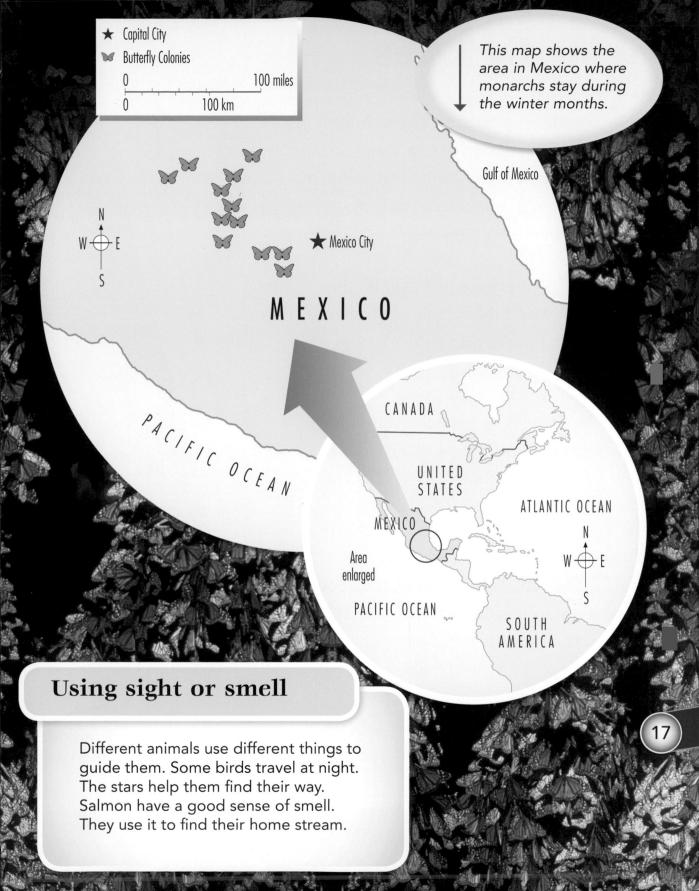

Capital City

Butterfly Colonies

0		100 miles
0	100 km	

This map shows the area in Mexico where monarchs stay during the winter months.

Gulf of Mexico

N
W ⊕ E
S

★ Mexico City

MEXICO

PACIFIC OCEAN

CANADA

UNITED STATES

MEXICO

Area enlarged

PACIFIC OCEAN

ATLANTIC OCEAN

N
W ⊕ E
S

SOUTH AMERICA

Using sight or smell

Different animals use different things to guide them. Some birds travel at night. The stars help them find their way. Salmon have a good sense of smell. They use it to find their home stream.

Butterfly Trees

It is November in Mexico. The **monarch** from the garden in Canada arrives (see map). So do millions of other monarchs. They gather high in the mountains. They fly from one spot to another. Soon they will settle in **oyamel** trees for the winter.

The oyamel forests are just right for the monarchs. The trees protect them from wind and rain. Fog keeps them from drying out.

Now, it is December. Clumps of old leaves hang from the trees. Where did the butterflies go? The air warms. A flash of orange appears. One of the leaves flutters away. The clumps are not leaves after all. They are butterflies!

During the winter, monarchs do not move much. The cool weather makes their bodies slow down. If it is below 55 °F (13 °C), monarchs cannot even fly. Being still means they do not need much food. But it also puts them in danger.

Monarchs in trees can look like dried leaves.

oyamel type of fir tree

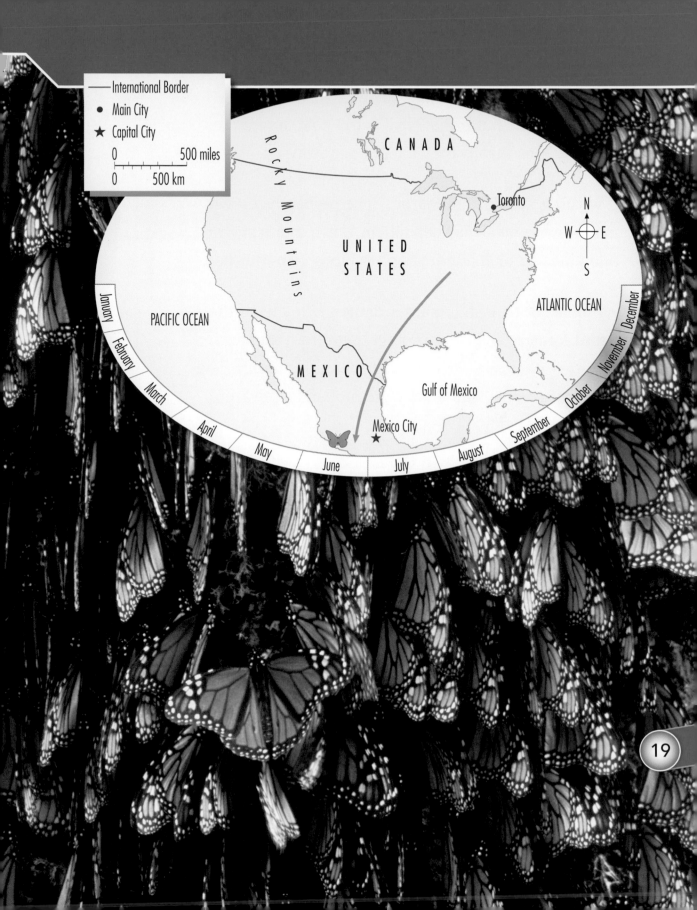

International Border
● Main City
★ Capital City

0   500 miles
0   500 km

CANADA

Rocky Mountains

UNITED
STATES

● Toronto

N
W ✦ E
S

PACIFIC OCEAN

ATLANTIC OCEAN

MEXICO

Gulf of Mexico

Mexico City
★

January
February
March
April
May
June
July
August
September
October
November
December

19

Winter dangers

Monarchs face many dangers in Mexico. Some birds and mice eat the butterflies. If it is too cold, monarchs cannot fly. This means they cannot get away.

Bad weather also kills monarchs. The monarchs crowd together in winter. This keeps them warm. But a storm in one place can kill hundreds of millions of butterflies.

The monarchs face still another danger. They need the **oyamel** forests. The trees protect them from rain and cold. Other places in Mexico are too hot or too dry. The forests are special. That is why the monarchs return to them each year.

But people are cutting down the forests. Without the trees, monarchs will have no winter homes. Many people are working to save the forests.

Some monarchs are eaten by mice and birds.

Winter crowding

In summer monarchs spread out. They live on more than 385,000 square miles (1 million square kilometers) of land. But in winter they crowd together in about a dozen spots. Added together the spots are smaller than 28 soccer fields!

The Trip Home

It is late February in Mexico. Winter is almost over. Soon the **monarchs** will start the journey north.

The monarchs begin to **mate**. Males and females join together. Then, the females lay eggs. Some mate before they leave their winter homes. Others wait until they start the trip home.

The monarch from Canada mates. Then, she flies north. She lays eggs on the way. She searches for a special plant. It is called **milkweed**. Her eggs will hatch into caterpillars. They will be hungry. Milkweed is the only plant they will eat.

So, she lays eggs on milkweed plants. She may lay 400 eggs over a wide area. She lays most of them in the southern United States (see map).

The monarch has lived a long life for a butterfly. On the trip back home to Canada, she dies. But her children are growing from the eggs she laid.

The monarchs leave Mexico in February and March.

milkweed type of plant monarch caterpillars eat

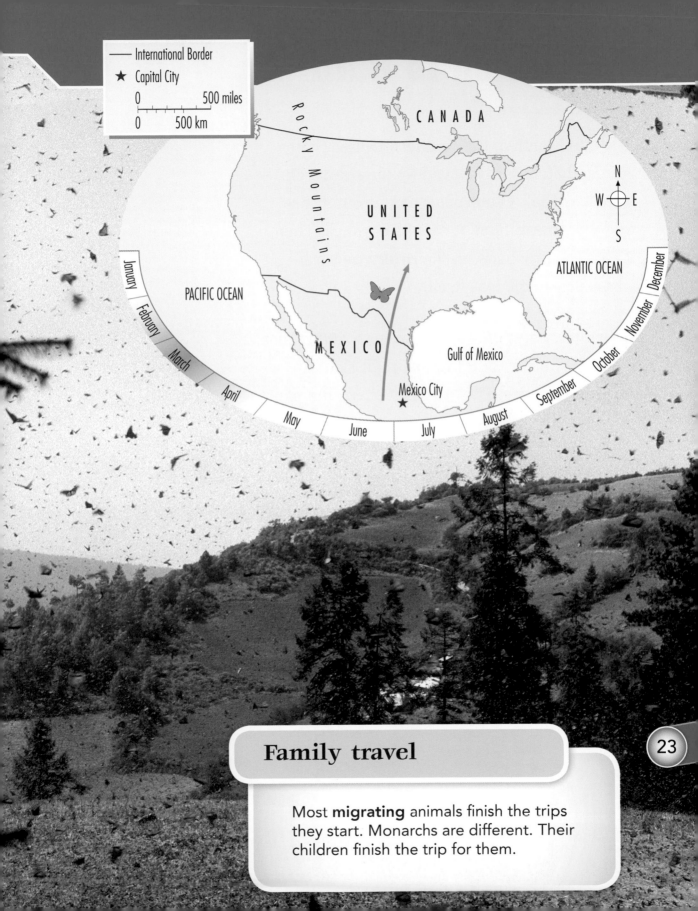

International Border

★ Capital City

0   500 miles

0   500 km

CANADA

Rocky Mountains

UNITED STATES

PACIFIC OCEAN

ATLANTIC OCEAN

MEXICO

Gulf of Mexico

Mexico City

N W E S

January February March April May June July August September October November December

Family travel

Most **migrating** animals finish the trips they start. Monarchs are different. Their children finish the trip for them.

A Monarch Is Born

It is late March in the southern United States. An egg hatches. It was laid by the **monarch** from Canada. A caterpillar comes out. It has one job: to eat! First, it eats its eggshell. Then, it eats the tiny hairs on the **milkweed** leaf. Then, it eats the leaf itself.

In just ten days, the caterpillar gets 2,000 times bigger. It quickly outgrows its tight skin. It **molts** five times. This means it sheds the old skin. A new skin waits beneath.

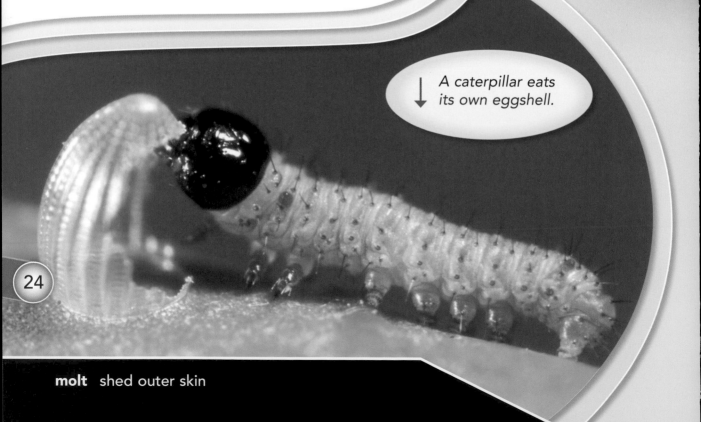

A caterpillar eats its own eggshell.

24

molt shed outer skin

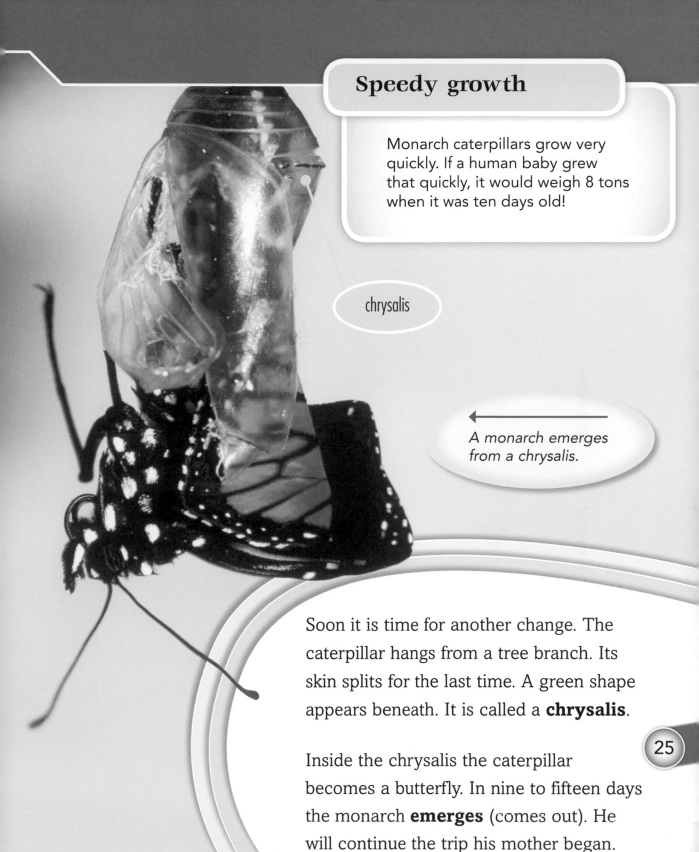

Speedy growth

Monarch caterpillars grow very quickly. If a human baby grew that quickly, it would weigh 8 tons when it was ten days old!

chrysalis

A monarch emerges from a chrysalis.

Soon it is time for another change. The caterpillar hangs from a tree branch. Its skin splits for the last time. A green shape appears beneath. It is called a **chrysalis**.

Inside the chrysalis the caterpillar becomes a butterfly. In nine to fifteen days the monarch **emerges** (comes out). He will continue the trip his mother began.

25

Journey's End

The new **monarch** comes out in April. He **mates**. The female he mates with lays eggs. He flies north, as the other monarchs do.

Finally, in May he arrives in Canada. He has never been there before. He may end up not far from where his mother was born.

Other monarchs stop in the northern United States. Some go to Canada. The **migration** cycle is finished. The monarchs have traveled from home and back again.

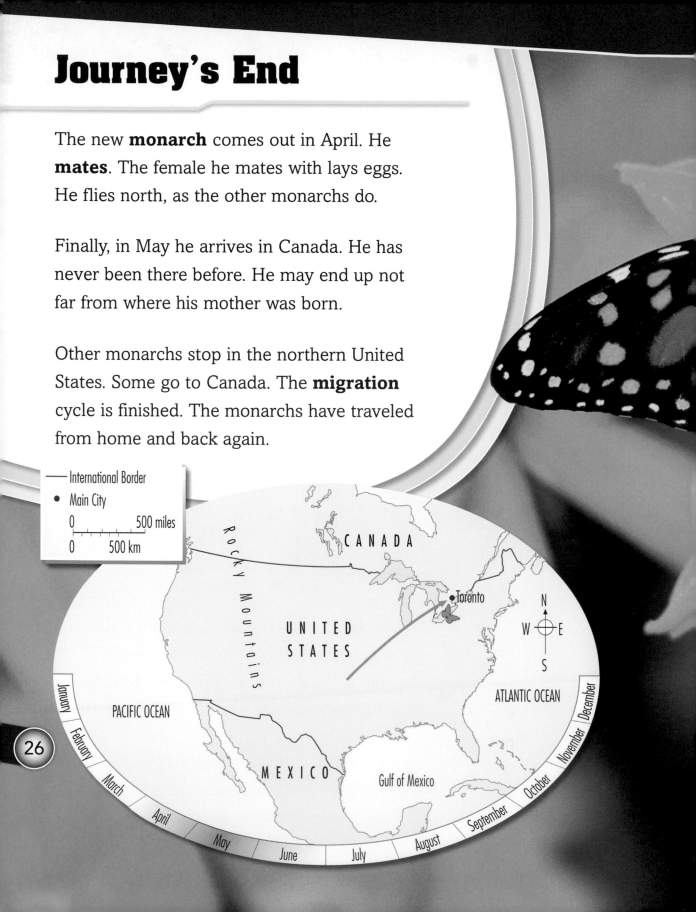

International Border

● Main City

0 — 500 miles

0 — 500 km

CANADA

Rocky Mountains

Toronto

N
W — E
S

UNITED STATES

ATLANTIC OCEAN

PACIFIC OCEAN

MEXICO

Gulf of Mexico

January, February, March, April, May, June, July, August, September, October, November, December

Monarchs that do not fly to Mexico live for about a month.

The monarch will live for about a month. His children and grandchildren will stay in the north. They will live about a month, too.

But his great-grandchildren will live much longer. They will make an amazing journey. They will fly all the way to Mexico.

Monarch Journeys

Each year **monarchs** travel to winter homes. Monarchs west of the Rocky Mountains go to spots on California's coast (see map on page 11). Monarchs east of the Rocky Mountains travel to forests in Mexico.

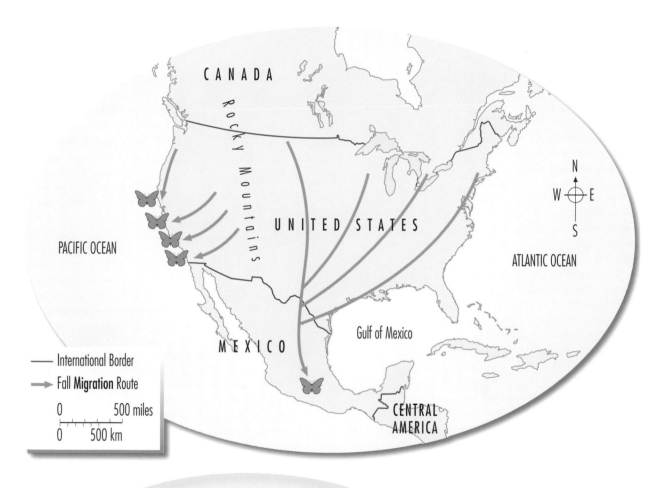

CANADA

Rocky Mountains

UNITED STATES

PACIFIC OCEAN

ATLANTIC OCEAN

N
W ⊕ E
S

Gulf of Mexico

MEXICO

CENTRAL AMERICA

— International Border
→ Fall **Migration** Route

| 0 | 500 miles |
| 0 | 500 km |

This is the route taken by butterflies during the fall. They are flying south to Mexico and west to California.

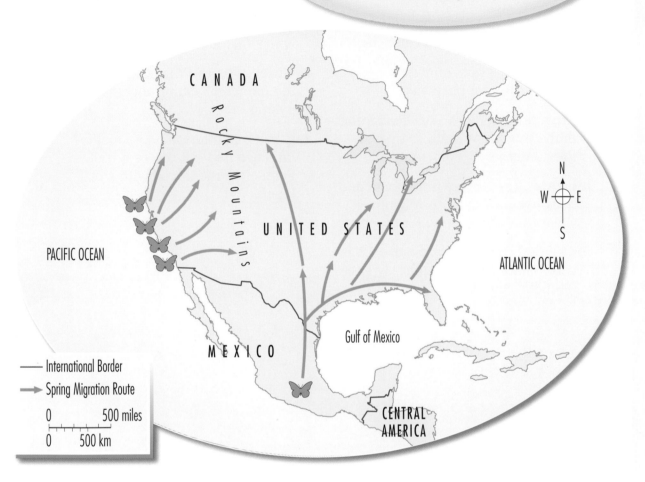

This is the route taken by monarchs in the spring. They are returning north to Canada and east to the Rocky Mountains.

CANADA

Rocky Mountains

UNITED STATES

PACIFIC OCEAN

ATLANTIC OCEAN

N
W—E
S

Gulf of Mexico

MEXICO

—— International Border
➤ Spring Migration Route

0   500 miles
0   500 km

CENTRAL
AMERICA

The monarchs from the east have a very long trip.
They sometimes fly 3,000 miles (4,800 kilometers).
In the spring, they begin to travel north. Their children
finish the trip for them.

Glossary

breed have offspring. Many animals migrate in order to breed.

chrysalis stage of life between caterpillar and butterfly. A monarch caterpillar turns into a chrysalis.

emerge come out. A monarch emerges from a chrysalis.

mate join together to have offspring. Some monarchs mate soon after they emerge.

migrate travel away from home and back again. Monarchs migrate to California and Mexico for the winter.

milkweed type of plant monarch caterpillars eat. Monarchs lay eggs on milkweed plants.

molt shed outer skin. A caterpillar molts several times in its life.

monarch type of orange-and-black butterfly. Monarch butterflies have wings that look like stained glass.

oyamel type of fir tree. In Mexico the monarchs clump together in oyamel trees.

tag put a marker on an animal or insect to find out where it travels. People tag monarchs with small labels.

Want to Know More?

Books to read

Hibbert, Clare. *Life of a Butterfly*. Chicago: Raintree, 2004.

Rea, Ba. *Monarch! Come Play with Me*. Glenshaw, PA: Bas Relief, 2006.

Rylant, Cynthia. *The Journey: Stories of Migration*. New York: Scholastic, 2006.

Websites

http://www.monarchwatch.org./
Find out a lot of information about monarchs and their migration.

http://www.learner.org/jnorth/
Kids observe migrating animals and share their information on this site.

Read more about the seasons in *The Day the Earth Stood Still*.

Find out more about amazing animals in *Animal Secrets*.

Index